I0827878

The Rite of

In the Extraordinary Form
With both English and Spanish Translations

El Rito del

Segun su Forma Extraordinaria
Con traducciones en ingles y español

Rev. Fr. J. Fryar FSSP

The Rite of Holy Baptism in the Extraordinary Form.

First Printing: 2018
Revised (with minor corrections): 2024
Revised 2026

Prepared and Published by Rev Fr J Fryar FSSP

Priestly Fraternity of St. Peter in Los Angeles
9710 White Oak Ave.,
Northridge CA 91325

email@fssp.la

http://FSSP.LA

Additional copies may be obtained on amazon.com or lulu.com

Also, by contacting the Priestly Fraternity of St. Peter of Los Angeles at the above address.

Contents

The Latin texts in this booklet have been taken from the Rituale Romanum of 1962. The English texts match the translation found in the 1950 Roman Ritual of Rev. Philip T. Weller.

For the Spanish texts we have used the text provided by the FSSP of Mexico.

The admonition regarding baptism in Spanish is taken from an appendix to the Rituale Romanum - *Ex Manuali Toletano*.

The front image is used courtesy of Windstar Embroidery Designs www.windstarembroidery.com

Other images in the book are taken from depositphotos.com

Special thanks to Rev. Fr. B. Austin FSSP for his assistance in review and proof reading.

Preface

With the growth of the Extraordinary Form throughout the world, we are moving beyond the photocopied pages that clutter pews and have need for dignified books with which we can follow the liturgy.

This present booklet is to help the attendees follow the sacred Rite of Baptism of Infants in the Extraordinary Form. We have used the English translation as is found in the Roman Ritual of Rev. Philip Weller (*Bruce Publishing Co. 1950*), because this is the Ritual that is most commonly used. While there is no official English translation of the 1962 liturgy, it is nice when the translation in the hands of the faithful matches that of the celebrant.

We have also included the ceremony in Spanish. There is a greater demand for Spanish as the years go by and this booklet gives the option for Spanish-speakers to follow along.

We have not included the ceremony of Baptism of an adult in this booklet, neither have we made distinctions for the baptism of multiple infants, since we did not want this booklet to become too large or cumbersome.

Finally, I humbly ask the reader to spare a prayer for me.

- Fr J Fryar FSSP

The Baptism Ceremony
For Infants

The ceremony begins outside the door of the church, where the celebrant, with his back to the church door, greets the family. After having (optionally) said a few words regarding the importance of this holy Sacrament, he asks the following questions to which the godparents respond in the name of the child.

N.., Quid petis ab Ecclesia Dei?
℟ Fidem.

N.., what dost thou ask of the Church of God?
℟ Faith.

Fides quid tibi praestat?
℟ Vitam aeternam.

What does faith bestow on thee?
℟ Life everlasting.

Si igitur vis ad vitam ingredi, serva mandata. Diliges Dominum Deum tuum ex toto corde tuo, et ex tota anima tua, et ex tota mente tua, et proximum tuum sicut teipsum.

If then thou wilt enter into life, keep the commandments: thou shall love the Lord thy God with thy whole heart, and with thy whole soul, and with thy whole mind, and thy neighbor as thyself.

The celebrant then gently blows three times on the face of the child, and says:

Exi ab eo *(ea)*, immunde spiritus, et da locum Spiritui Sancto Paraclito.

Go out from him *(her)*, thou unclean spirit, and make way for the Holy Spirit, the Consoler.

The celebrant makes the sign of the cross with his thumb on the forehead and over the heart of the child as he says:

Receive the sign of the Cross upon thy ✠ brow and upon thy ✠ heart. Enter into the service of the heavenly commandments, and be thou such in thy conduct that thou mayest deserve henceforth to be known as God's temple.

Accipe signum crucis tam in fron ✠ te, quam in cor ✠ de, sume fidem caelestium praeceptorum: et talis esto moribus, ut templum Dei iam esse possis.

Let us pray.
Graciously hear our entreaty, O Lord, we beseech thee, and with thine unfailing might guard thy chosen one, N..., now signed with the seal of our Lord's holy cross. Help him *(her)* to hold fast to this first acquaintance with thy majestic glory, that in keeping thy commandments, he *(she)* may deserve to attain the everlasting bliss destined for all who are born anew. Through Christ our Lord.
℟ Amen.

Oremus.
Preces nostras, quaesumus, Domine, clementer exaudi; et hunc electum tuum *(hanc electam tuam)*, N..., crucis Dominicae impressione signatum *(-am)*, perpetua virtute custodi; ut, magnitudinis gloriae tuae rudimenta servans, per custodiam mandatorum tuorum, ad regenerationis gloriam pervenire mereatur. Per Christum Dominum nostrum.
℟ Amen.

Laying his hand upon the head of the child, he then raises his hand a little and continues:

Oremus.
Omnipotens, sempiterne Deus, Pater Domini nostri Iesu Christi, respicere dignare super hunc famulum tuum *(hanc famulam tuam)*, N.., quem *(quam)* ad rudimenta fidei vocare dignatus es; omnem caecitatem cordis ab eo *(ea)* expelle; disrumpe omnes laqueos Satanae, quibus fuerat colligatus *(-a)*; aperi ei, Domine, ianuam pietatis tuae, ut, signo sapientiae tuae imbutus *(-a)*, omnium cupiditatum foetoribus careat, et ad suavem odorem praeceptorum tuorum laetus *(-a)* tibi in Ecclesia tua deserviat, et proficiat de die in diem. Per eundem Christum Dominum nostrum.
℟ Amen.

Let us pray.
Almighty, everlasting God, Father of our Lord, Jesus Christ! Deign to regard with favor thy servant *(handmaid)* N.., whom it has pleased thee to call to the beginnings of faith. Drive out from him *(her)* all blindness of heart. Sunder all snares of Satan which hitherto bound him *(her)*; open to him *(her)* the gate of thy fatherly love, that dedicated with the seal of thy wisdom, he *(she)* may remain unsullied from every evil desire. And inspired by the loveliness of thy precepts, may he *(she)* serve thee with glad heart in thy Church, advancing in perfection from day to day. Through the selfsame Christ our Lord.
℟ Amen.

If the salt has not been blessed, the celebrant then blesses it. If it is already blessed, the following prayer is omitted.

I purge thee of evil, thou creature of salt, in the name of God ✠ the Father almighty, and in the love of Jesus ✠ Christ, our Lord, and by the power of the Holy ✠ Spirit. I exorcise thee by the living ✠ God, by the true ✠ God, by the holy ✠ God, by God ✠ who did provide thee in preservation of human needs, and did command that thou be consecrated by His servants for the people coming unto Faith, that in the name of the Blessed Trinity thou mayest become an outward sign of salvation, repulsing the enemy. Therefore, we beseech thee, O Lord, our God, to sanctify ✠ with thy sanctifying power, to bless ✠ with thy benediction this creature of salt, that it may be for all who receive it a sure remedy, even enduring within them; in the name of the selfsame Jesus Christ, our Lord, Who shall come to judge the living and the dead and the world by fire.

℟ Amen.

Exorcizo te, creatura salis, in nomine Dei ✠ Patris omnipotentis, et in caritate Domini nostri Iesu ✠ Christi, et in virtute Spiritus ✠ Sancti. Exorcizo te per Deum ✠ vivum, per Deum ✠ verum, per Deum ✠ sanctum, per Deum, ✠ qui te ad tutelam humani generis procreavit, et populo venienti ad credulitatem per servos suos consecrari praecepit, ut in nomine sanctae Trinitatis efficiaris salutare sacramentum ad effugandum inimicum.

Proinde rogamus te, Domine Deus noster, ut hanc creaturam salis sanctificando sancti ✠ fices, et benedicendo bene ✠ dicas, ut fiat omnibus accipientibus perfecta medicina, permanens in visceribus eorum, in nomine eiusdem Domini nostri Iesu Christi, qui venturus est iudicare vivos et mortuos, et saeculum per ignem.

℟ Amen.

He then places a small amount of salt on the tongue of the child, as the first taste of blessed food.

N.., accipe sal sapientiae: propitiatio sit tibi in vitam aeternam.
℟ Amen.

N.., receive the salt of wisdom. May it be unto thee a sign of reconciliation unto life everlasting.
℟ Amen.

Pax tecum.
℟ Et cum spiritu tuo.

Peace be with you
℟ And with your spirit.

Oremus.
Deus patrum nostrorum, Deus universae conditor veritatis, te supplices exoramus, ut hunc famulum tuum *(hanc famulam tuam)*, N.., respicere digneris propitius, et hoc primum pabulum salis gustantem, non diutius esurire permittas, quo minus cibo expleatur caelesti, quatenus sit semper spiritu fervens, spe gaudens, tuo semper nomini serviens.

Let us pray.
God of our fathers, O God, thou source of all truth, humbly we implore thee to look with mercy upon this thy servant *(handmaid)*, N.., and no more let him *(her)* hunger who now tastes this first nourishment of salt. But let him *(her)* be enriched with heavenly food, so that he *(she)* may ever be inflamed with zeal, joyous in hope, constant in serving thee.

Perduc eum *(eam)*, Domine, quaesumus, ad novae regenerationis lavacrum, ut cum fidelibus tuis promissionum tuarum aeterna praemia consequi mereatur. Per Christum Dominum nostrum.
℟ Amen.

We bid thee, Lord, lead him *(her)* to the bath where one is born anew, that in the company of thy faithful he *(she)* may deserve to win the everlasting reward which thou hast promised. Through Christ our Lord.
℟ Amen.

He addresses the Evil One, telling him to depart from this holy candidate for baptism and never to return, nor to violate the holy Seal of the Cross with which the child is blessed on his forehead.

I cast thee out, unclean spirit, in the name of the Father, ✠ and of the Son, ✠ and of the Holy ✠ Spirit. Depart and vanish from this servant of God, N..: For it is He Who commands thee, thou doomed and accursed one, He Whose feet once trod the waves, Who reached out His saving hand to Peter when he began to sink.

Exorcizo te, immunde spiritus, in nomine Patris, ✠ et Filii, ✠ et Spiritus ✠ Sancti, ut exeas, et recedas ab hoc famulo *(hac famula)* Dei N..: Ipse enim tibi imperat, maledicte damnate, qui pedibus super mare ambulavit, et Petro mergenti dexteram porrexit.

Therefore, accursed fiend, admit thy doom, and pay honor to Jesus Christ, His Son and to the Holy Spirit, and keep far from this servant *(handmaid)* of God, N…, for Jesus Christ, our Lord and God, has graciously called him *(her)* to His holy grace and blessing, indeed, to the fountain of baptism.

Ergo, maledicte diabole, recognosce sententiam tuam, et da honorem Deo vivo et vero, da honorem Iesu Christo Filio eius, et Spiritui Sancto, et recede ab hoc famulo *(hac famula)* Dei N…, quia istum *(-am)* sibi Deus, et Dominus noster Iesus Christus ad suam sanctam gratiam, et benedictionem, fontemque Baptismatis vocare dignatus est.

Here the celebrant signs the forehead of the child saying:

Et hoc signum sanctae Crucis, ✠ quod nos fronti eius damus, tu, maledicte diabole, numquam audeas violare. Per eundem Christum Dominum nostrum.

℟ Amen.

And this sign of the holy ✠ Cross which we trace on his *(her)* brow, do thou, accursed demon, never dare to violate. Through the selfsame Christ our Lord.

℟ Amen.

Placing his hand on the head of the child, he then raises his hand a little and continues:

Oremus.
Aeternam, ac iustissimam pietatem tuam deprecor, Domine sancte, Pater omnipotens, aeterne Deus, auctor luminis et veritatis, super hunc famulum tuum *(hanc famulam tuam)* N.., ut digneris eum *(eam)* illuminare lumine intelligentiae tuae: munda eum *(eam)*, et sanctifica: da ei scientiam veram, ut, dignus *(-a)* gratia Baptismi tui effectus *(-a)*, teneat firmam spem, consilium rectum, doctrinam sanctam. Per Christum Dominum nostrum.

℟ Amen.

Let us pray.
O holy Lord, almighty Father, eternal God, Author of light and truth, I entreat for this thy servant *(handmaid)*, N.., thine unfailing and righteous mercy. May it please thee to enlighten him *(her)* with the light of thine understanding. Cleanse and sanctify him *(her)*. Endow him *(her)* with true knowledge, so that he *(she)* may be made worthy of the grace of thy baptism, and thus remain steadfast in firm hope, right purpose, and holy doctrine. Through Christ our Lord.

℟ Amen.

The celebrant now leads the child into the church by the edge of his stole. All follow and as they enter everyone recites the Creed and the Our Father. The celebrant stops before arriving at the baptistry, and stands with his back to the baptistry.

N.., enter into the temple of God, that thou mayest have part with Christ unto life everlasting.

℟ Amen.

N.., ingredere in templum Dei, ut habeas partem cum Christo in vitam aeternam.

℟ Amen.

I believe in God, the Father almighty, Creator of heaven and earth; and in Jesus Christ, His only Son, our Lord: who was conceived by the Holy Ghost, born of the Virgin Mary, suffered under Pontius Pilate, was crucified, died, and was buried. He descended into hell; the third day He rose again from the dead; He ascended into heaven, sitteth at the right hand of God, the Father Almighty. From thence He shall come to judge the living and the dead. I believe in the Holy Ghost, the holy catholic Church, the communion of saints, the forgiveness of sins, the resurrection of the body, and life everlasting. Amen.

Credo in Deum, Patrem omnipotentem, Creatorem caeli et terrae. Et in Iesum Christum, Filium eius unicum, Dominum nostrum: qui conceptus est de Spiritu Sancto, natus ex Maria Virgine, passus sub Pontio Pilato, crucifixus, mortuus, et sepultus: descendit ad inferos; tertia die resurrexit a mortuis; ascendit ad caelos; sedet ad dexteram Dei Patris omnipotentis; inde venturus est iudicare vivos et mortuos. Credo in Spiritum Sanctum, sanctam Ecclesiam catholicam, Sanctorum communionem, remissionem peccatorum, carnis resurrectionem, vitam aeternam. Amen.

Pater noster, qui es in caelis, sanctificetur nomen tuum. Adveniat regnum tuum. Fiat voluntas tua, sicut in caelo, et in terra. Panem nostrum quotidianum da nobis hodie. Et dimitte nobis debita nostra, sicut et nos dimittimus debitoribus nostris. Et ne nos inducas in tentationem: sed libera nos a malo. Amen.

Our Father, Who art in heaven, hallowed be Thy name; Thy kingdom come; Thy will be done on earth as it is in heaven. Give us this day our daily bread; and forgive us our trespasses, as we forgive those who trespass against us; and lead us not into temptation, but deliver us from evil. Amen.

The celebrant again pronounces an exorcism over the devil, telling him to leave this child of God.

Exorcizo te, omnis spiritus immunde in nomine Dei ✠ Patris omnipotentis, et in nomine Iesu ✠ Christi Filii eius, Domini et Iudicis nostri, et in virtute Spiritus ✠ Sancti, ut discedas ab hoc plasmate Dei N.., quod Dominus noster ad templum sanctum suum vocare dignatus est, ut fiat templum Dei vivi, et Spiritus Sanctus habitet in eo. Per eundum Christum Dominum nostrum, qui venturus est iudicare vivos et mortuos, et saeculum per ignem.

℟ Amen.

I expel thee, every unclean spirit, in the name of God ✠ the Father almighty, in the name of Jesus ✠ Christ, His Son, our Lord and Judge, and by the power of the Holy ✠ Spirit. Depart from this handiwork of God N.., whom our Lord has deigned to call to His holy temple, that he *(she)* may be made a temple of the living God, and the Holy Spirit may dwell within him *(her)*. Through the selfsame Christ our Lord, Who shall come to judge the living and the dead and the world by fire.

℟ Amen.

Moistening his thumb with saliva (this is optional if there is a fear of germs), he then blesses the ears and the nostrils of the child as he says:

Ephpheta, which means: Be thou opened! Unto the odor of sweetness. But thou, evil spirit, begone, for the judgement of God draws nigh!

Ephpheta, quod est, Adaperire. In odorem suavitatis. Tu autem effugare, diabole; appropinquabit enim iudicium Dei.

He then questions the godparents again in the name of the child.

N.., dost thou renounce Satan?
℟ I do renounce him.

And all his works?
℟ I do renounce them.

And all his allurements?
℟ I do renounce them.

N.., abrenuntias Satanae?
℟ Abrenuntio.

Et omnibus operibus eius?
℟ Abrenuntio.

Et omnibus pompis eius?
℟ Abrenuntio.

Here the celebrant anoints the child on the back and on the chest with the Oil of the Catechumens

I anoint thee ✠ with the oil of salvation, in Christ Jesus our Lord, that thou mayest have life everlasting.
℟ Amen.

Ego te linio ✠ oleo salutis in Christo Iesu Domino nostro, ut habeas vitam aeternam.
℟ Amen.

Now all enter the baptistry, where the celebrant changes from a purple to a white stole. If the godparents are not holding the child, they need to do so at this point.

The celebrant then questions the godparents a final time.

N.., credis in Deum Patrem omnipotentem, creatorem caeli et terrae?
℟ Credo.

N.., dost thou believe in God, the Father almighty, Creator of heaven and earth?
℟ I do believe.

Credis in Iesum Christum, Filium eius unicum, Dominum nostrum, natum, et passum?
℟ Credo.

Dost thou believe in Jesus Christ, his Sole-Begotten Son, our Lord, Who was born unto us and Who suffered for us?
℟ I do believe.

Credis et in Spiritum sanctum, sanctam Ecclesiam Catholicam, Sanctorum communionem, remissionem peccatorum, carnis resurrectionem, et vitam aeternam?
℟ Credo.

Dost thou believe in the Holy Spirit, the holy Catholic Church, the communion of saints, the forgiveness of sins, the resurrection of the body, and life everlasting?
℟ I do believe.

This final question clarifies that the desire for baptism is a positive act of the will.

N.., vis baptizari?
℟ Volo.

N.., wilt thou be baptized?
℟. I will.

The godparents hold the child over the baptismal font in such a way that the priest may pour the water across the forehead of the child.

The celebrant pours the water three times in the form of a cross over the forehead of the child as he says the following. *This is the matter and form of the sacrament.*

N.., I baptize thee in the name of the Father ✠ and of the Son ✠, and of the Holy ✠ Spirit.

N.., Ego te baptizo in nomine ✠ Patris, fundit primo, **et Filii ✠,** fundit secundo, **et Spiritus ✠ Sancti.** fundit tertio.

He then anoints the head of the child with Holy Chrism.

May God almighty, Father of our Lord Jesus Christ, Who has caused thee to be born anew by water and the Holy Spirit, and granted thee remission of all sins, may He anoint ✠ thee with the chrism of salvation in the selfsame Christ Jesus, our Lord, unto life everlasting.
℟ Amen.

Deus omnipotens, Pater Domini nostri Iesu Christi, qui te regeneravit ex aqua et Spiritu Sancto, quique dedit tibi remissionem omnium peccatorum (hic inungit), ipse te ✠ liniat Chrismate Salutis in eodem Christo Iesu Domino nostro in vitam aeternam.
℟ Amen.

Peace be with you.
℟ And with your spirit.

Pax tibi.
℟ Et cum spiritu tuo.

He places a white garment over the child.

Accipe vestem candidam, quam perferas immaculatam ante tribunal Domini nostri Iesu Christi, ut habeas vitam aeternam.
℟ Amen.

Receive this white garment, and carry it unsullied unto the judgment seat of our Lord, Jesus Christ, that thou mayest have life everlasting.
℟ Amen.

He presents the godfather with a burning candle.

Accipe lampadem ardentem, et irreprehensibilis custodi Baptismum tuum: serva Dei mandata, ut, cum Dominus venerit ad nuptias, possis occurrere ei una cum omnibus Sanctis in aula caelesti, et vivas in saecula saeculorum.
℟ Amen.

Receive this burning light. Safeguard thy baptism by a blameless life. Keep the commandments of God, that when our Lord shall come for the heavenly nuptials thou mayest meet Him together with all the saints in the court of heaven, and live forever and ever.
℟ Amen.

N.., vade in pace, et Dominus sit tecum.
℟ Amen.

N.., go in peace, and the Lord be with you.
℟ Amen.

The Dedication of a Child to Our Lady

AFTER THE RECEPTION OF HOLY BAPTISM

Composed by Father Noël le Mire, S.M. and adapted by Father William Cole, S.M.

blessed Virgin Mary our Mother, when the Son of God decided to take upon Himself our human life in order that we might share in His Divine Life, He did not wish to come to us without your free cooperation. He deliberately willed to have need of you.

Look down today from heaven upon little N... He (*she*) has received from his *(her)* parents the life of man, and now by the Holy Sacrament of Baptism, he (*she*) has been given a life which is infinitely superior, a share in the very life of God. We know that just as God is his *(her)* Father and our Father, you are, in regard to his *(her)* spiritual life, his *(her)* Mother and our Mother.

We confide this child to you. Show yourself his *(her)* Mother. Watch over his *(her)* education; nourish him *(her)* with the life of grace; make him *(her)* progress in his *(her)* Christian life just as his *(her)* human parents aid him *(her)* to progress in the physical as well as spiritual life.

Protect the precious life which has just been received. Be for him *(her)* a real Mother to guard him *(her)* in your arms when the devil seeks to destroy his *(her)* spiritual life in your son Jesus Christ. May he *(her)* love you as Jesus Christ loved you, for our love for you is nothing else but a participation in the love of your Son for you.

In the name of N.., we wish to make today his *(her)* first prayer to his *(her)* heavenly Mother:

(All recite the) Hail Mary...

Regarding Baptism

ur Divine Master is quite clear in the Sacred Scriptures that without baptism we cannot be saved. (*Mk 16:16*)

At baptism all our sins including original sin are washed away in the Blood of our Redeemer and our souls are filled with sanctifying grace - the very dwelling of the Life of the Trinity within us.

Together with sanctifying grace, the Holy Ghost infuses in our souls the moral and theological virtues and all the gifts of the Holy Ghost. These are properties of habitual grace and proximate principles of supernatural action for the Christian.

Baptism also leaves an indelible mark on our soul. In other words it gives our soul a character that cannot be deleted, ever. This character is that we are born again by our Savior's death as a child of God, enabling us to receive the other sacraments and consecrating us for Christian religious worship.

Finally it is by the reception of this sacrament that we become members of the Catholic Church.

If we preserve the graces that we receive at baptism, we have the guarantee of Heaven after our duration on earth. Sadly, however, the state of sanctifying grace is lost when we commit mortal sin. While we cannot receive the sacrament of baptism more than once, we are able to restore sanctifying grace to our souls by having our sins forgiven in the sacrament of confession.

Baptism is the most important of all the sacraments. Without it we cannot enter Heaven. Without it we cannot receive any other sacrament. Without sanctifying grace, which we receive at baptism, we cannot obtain merit for any good deed. For these reasons it is imperative that a child be baptized within the first few weeks after birth. Furthermore, it is important to preserve the graces you have received at baptism in your soul as best as possible, striving to avoid mortal sin, and if you commit mortal sin, to go to confession at your soonest convenience.

or baptism to be valid, certain things are necessary. First, you need a *candidate*. This candidate needs to have faith. For a child, this faith is provided by the godparents who profess the faith for him and commit to assuring that as the child grows he will learn this faith.

Next, a *minister* is needed. The usual minister of baptism is a priest, and usually the pastor of the parish has the right to baptize his spiritual children. A deacon may also administer baptism, or, of course, a bishop.

In the case of emergency (for example imminent death) any person can baptize, even someone who is not Catholic, provided that he or she has the intention to administer the sacrament according to the mind of the Church. In such circumstances no ceremonies are performed except the actual form: *"I baptize you in the name of the Father and of the Son and of the Holy Ghost"* while pouring natural water over the forehead of the candidate.

Then, as for all sacraments, *matter* and *form* is required. The matter for baptism is a washing with water. For the solemn ceremony of baptism this baptismal water is specially blessed and infused with sacred chrism and holy oil. This blessing usually takes place at the Easter Vigil.

The form of baptism are the words that the celebrant pronounces as he pours the water: *"N.., I baptize you in the name of the Father and of the Son and of the Holy Ghost."* Note that for the baptism to be valid, the same minister has to pour the water and say the words.

he ceremony begins outside the church. We get a visual image of the reality, that the unbaptized soul is not within the fold of the church. Outside these doors several things happen. The child is asked questions that the godparents answer for him or her. Then the child receives his first blessing, a sign of the cross on the brow - and then the devil is told not to dare abuse that sign with which the child was sealed. The child also received his first spiritual nourishment - a small amount of blessed salt. There are many blessed foods in the Catholic Church, the most important of which is Christ Himself, our spiritual food in the Blessed Sacrament.

Finally the child is led by the end of the priest's stole into the church. As the priest guides the child into the church today, so also will he lead him out at the end of his life, when he accompanies the coffin to the hearse. From there, God willing, the angels will take him to Heaven.

As everyone enters into the church they recite the Creed and the Our Father. The Creed to profess our faith, and the Our Father as the perfect prayer that Our Divine Master taught us.

The procession stops outside the baptistry of the church. Traditionally the baptistry is at the rear of the church. If such is the case at your church, the procession doesn't enter all the way into the nave, but just into the rear of the church where the baptistry is.

Outside the baptistry the priest will begin with another exorcism, and will anoint the child with Holy Oil on the child's front and on his back. It's good for the godparents to be ready to undo the top button (or two) of the child's garment when it comes time for this.

At the font the godparents once again answer questions for the candidate, and then the child is baptized. After the baptism we have an anointing with Sacred Chrism on the head of the child; the clothing with the white garment symbolizing the purity of soul after baptism and finally the godparents are given a burning candle. This candle represents the fact that we should shine the light of Christ by our good actions as our Divine Master bids us in the Gospels: "So let your light shine before men, that they may see your good works and glorify your Father who is in Heaven." (*Mt 5:16*)

A Note to the Godparents

It is an honor to be a godparent. It is a privilege which carries with it obligations. You make the profession of faith for your godchild on the day of baptism, and by doing so, you accept the obligation of assuring that this child will profess this faith throughout his or her life.

The Catholic Church requires that a godparent be a Catholic of exceptional caliber. Someone who can be a role model for a new Catholic to imitate. You need to be attending Mass at least every week. Going to confession. Living in a valid marriage or living a chaste life. Confirmed. You need to know your faith.

If you find yourself not being the Catholic you should be, now is the time to step up to live the Faith you profess. Your godchild needs to see you live how a Catholic needs to live.

It is your obligation, furthermore, to guarantee that your godchild *learns* his or her faith and *lives* his or her faith. Usually the parents will take care of this formation. If such be the case, then you merely watch at a distance and let the parents teach their child. If, however, the parents do not raise the child Catholic or something happens to the parents, you need to do what you can within the boundaries of prudence, to make sure the child learns and lives the Faith.

In the event that as an adult your godchild drifts away, never rest from praying, doing sacrifices and urging by your words and example that he or she return to the practice of their religion and come back to a life of grace.

May God bless you in this endeavor, and may you remain faithful to these obligations.

El Rito del

Según su Forma Extraordinaria

La Ceremonia del Bautismo
PARA NIÑOS

Empezando afuera de la puerta principal de la iglesia, el sacerdote, espaldas hacia la puerta, puede decir unas palabras sobre este santo sacramento. Luego, interrogando a los padrinos, ellos contestan de parte del niño.

N.., Quid petis ab Ecclesia Dei?
℟ Fidem.

N.., ¿Qué pides a la Iglesia de Dios?
℟: La fe.

Fides quid tibi praestat?
℟ Vitam aeternam.

¿Qué te alcanza la fe?
℟: La vida eterna.

Si igitur vis ad vitam ingredi, serva mandata. Diliges Dominum Deum tuum ex toto corde tuo, et ex tota anima tua, et ex tota mente tua, et proximum tuum sicut teipsum.

Si quieres, pues, entrar a la vida eterna, cumple los mandamientos. Amarás al Señor tu Dios con todo tu corazón, con toda tu alma y con toda tu mente y al prójimo como a ti mismo.

El sacerdote sopla suavemente en la cara del niño diciendo:

Exi ab eo *(ea)*, immunde spiritus, et da locum Spiritui Sancto Paraclito.

Retírate de él *(ella)*, espíritu inmundo, y da el lugar al Espíritu Santo Paráclito.

Luego haciendo la señal de la Cruz sobre la frente y el pecho del niño, dice:

Accipe signum crucis tam in fron ✠ te, quam in cor ✠ de, sume fidem caelestium praeceptorum: et talis esto

Recibe el signo de la cruz en tu frente ✠ y en tu corazón ✠; sé fiel a los mandamientos divinos y vive de tal manera que desde ahora puedas ser templo de Dios.

moribus, ut templum Dei iam esse possis.

Oremos.
Te rogamos, Señor, que escuches benignamente nuestras preces, y a este elegido*(a)*, N..., signado*(a)* con la señal de la cruz del Señor, guárdale con tu perpetuo poder, para que, conservando siempre la primera señal de la grandeza de tu gloria, por la observancia de tus mandamientos merezca llegar a la gloria de la resurrección. Por Cristo nuestro Señor.
℟: Amen.

Oremus.
Preces nostras, quaesumus, Domine, clementer exaudi; et hunc electum tuum *(hanc electam tuam)*, N..., crucis Dominicae impressione signatum *(-am)*, perpetua virtute custodi; ut, magnitudinis gloriae tuae rudimenta servans, per custodiam mandatorum tuorum, ad regenerationis gloriam pervenire mereatur. Per Christum Dominum nostrum.
℟ Amen.

Extendiendo su mano sobre la cabeza del niño, y luego manteniéndola levantada, sigue:

Oremos.
Omnipotente y sempiterno Dios, Padre de nuestro Señor Jesucristo, dígnate mirar a este tu siervo*(a)* N.., a quien te has dignado llamar a los rudimentos de la fe; expulsa de él *(ella)* toda ceguera de corazón, rompe en él *(ella)* todos los lazos de Satanás con que estuvo atado*(a)*; ábrele*(la)*, Señor, las puertas

Oremus.
Omnipotens, sempiterne Deus, Pater Domini nostri Iesu Christi, respicere dignare super hunc famulum tuum *(hanc famulam tuam)*, N.., quem *(quam)* ad rudimenta fidei vocare dignatus es; omnem caecitatem cordis ab eo *(ea)* expelle; disrumpe omnes laqueos Satanae, quibus fuerat colligatus *(-a)*;

aperi ei, Domine, ianuam pietatis tuae, ut, signo sapientiae tuae imbutus *(-a)*, omnium cupiditatum foetoribus careat, et ad suavem odorem praeceptorum tuorum laetus *(-a)* tibi in Ecclesia tua deserviat, et proficiat de die in diem. Per eundem Christum Dominum nostrum.

℟ Amen.

de tu piedad, para que, imbuido*(a)* en la señal de tu sabiduría, se vea libre de todo hedor de la concupiscencia y, atraído*(a)* por el suave olor de tus mandamientos, te sirva alegre en tu Iglesia y adelante de día en día.

℟: Amén.

Después el sacerdote bendice, si no está de antemano bendecida, la sal:

Exorcizo te, creatura salis, in nomine Dei ✠ Patris omnipotentis, et in caritate Domini nostri Iesu ✠ Christi, et in virtute Spiritus ✠ Sancti. Exorcizo te per Deum ✠ vivum, per Deum ✠ verum, per Deum ✠ sanctum, per Deum, ✠ qui te ad tutelam humani generis procreavit, et populo venienti ad credulitatem per servos suos consecrari praecepit, ut in nomine sanctae Trinitatis efficiaris salutare sacramentum ad effugandum inimicum.

Te conjuro, sal, en el nombre de Dios ✠ Padre todopoderoso, en el amor de nuestro Señor ✠ Jesucristo y en la fuerza del Espíritu ✠ Santo. Te conjuro por el Dios ✠ vivo, por el Dios ✠ verdadero, por el Dios ✠ santo, por el Dios ✠ que te creó para protección del hombre y mandó que fueras consagrada por sus siervos para uso del pueblo que llega a la fe, a fin de que, en el nombre de la Trinidad santa, te conviertas en signo de salvación para ahuyentar al enemigo.

Por eso te rogamos, Señor, Dios nuestro, que santifiques ✠ y bendigas ✠ copiosamente esta sal, para que sirva de remedio eficaz a cuantos lo reciban y permanezcan en sus entrañas. Te lo pedimos en el nombre de nuestro Señor Jesucristo, que ha de venir a juzgar a vivos y a muertos, y al mundo por el fuego.

℟: Amén.

Proinde rogamus te, Domine Deus noster, ut hanc creaturam salis sanctificando sancti ✠ fices, et benedicendo bene ✠ dicas, ut fiat omnibus accipientibus perfecta medicina, permanens in visceribus eorum, in nomine eiusdem Domini nostri Iesu Christi, qui venturus est iudicare vivos et mortuos, et saeculum per ignem.

℟ Amen.

El sacerdote pone un poquito de sal bendecida en la boca del infante, siendo su primer gusto de comida bendecida.

N.., recibe la sal de la sabiduría, que te sirva para la vida eterna.
℟: Amén.

N.., accipe sal sapientiae: propitiatio sit tibi in vitam aeternam.
℟ Amen.

La paz sea contigo.
℟: y con tu espíritu.

Pax tecum.
℟ Et cum spiritu tuo.

Oremos.
Dios de nuestros padres, Dios autor de toda verdad, te pedimos suplicantes que te dignes mirar propicio a este siervo tuyo *(esta sierva tuya)* N.., y no permitas que el *(ella)* que gusta por primera ves

Oremus.
Deus patrum nostrorum, Deus universae conditor veritatis, te supplices exoramus, ut hunc famulum tuum *(hanc famulam tuam)*, N.., respicere digneris propitius, et hoc primum

pabulum salis gustantem, non diutius esurire permittas, quo minus cibo expleatur caelesti, quatenus sit semper spiritu fervens, spe gaudens, tuo semper nomini serviens.

Perduc eum *(eam)*, Domine, quaesumus, ad novae regenerationis lavacrum, ut cum fidelibus tuis promissionum tuarum aeterna praemia consequi mereatur. Per Christum Dominum nostrum.
℟ Amen.

esta sal, sufra por más tiempo el hambre, siendo privado*(a)* de este manjar celestial; antes sea siempre fervoroso*(a)* de espíritu, lleno*(a)* de la consoladora esperanza y perpetuo servidor de tu nombre.
Llévale*(la)*, Señor, te lo suplicamos, al lavatorio de la nueva regeneración para que merezca conseguir con tus fieles los premios eternos de tus promesas. Por Cristo nuestro Señor.
℟: Amén.

El sacerdote pronuncia después el siguiente exorcismo:

Exorcizo te, immunde spiritus, in nomine Patris, ✠ et Filii, ✠ et Spiritus ✠ Sancti, ut exeas, et recedas ab hoc famulo *(hac famula)* Dei N..: Ipse enim tibi imperat, maledicte damnate, qui pedibus super mare ambulavit, et Petro mergenti dexteram porrexit.

Ergo, maledicte diabole, recognosce sententiam tuam, et da honorem Deo vivo et vero, da honorem Iesu Christo Filio eius, et Spiritui Sancto, et

Exorcízote, inmundo espíritu, en el nombre del ✠ Padre, y del Hijo ✠, y del Espíritu ✠ Santo, para que salgas y te alejes de este siervo *(esta sierva)* de Dios, N..., pues te lo ordena, maldito condenado, Aquel que con sus pies caminó sobre el mar y dio su mano a Pedro que se hundía.

Reconoce, pues, maldito diablo, tu sentencia y da honor al Dios vivo y verdadero, da honor a Jesucristo, su Hijo y al

Espíritu Santo, y aléjate de este siervo *(esta sierva)* de Dios, N..., a quien Dios nuestro Señor ha dignado llamar a su santa gracia y bendición y a la fuente bautismal.

recede ab hoc famulo *(hac famula)* Dei N..., quia istum *(-am)* sibi Deus, et Dominus noster Iesus Christus ad suam sanctam gratiam, et benedictionem, fontemque Baptismatis vocare dignatus est.

Y tú, maldito diablo, no atrevas jamás profanar esta señal de la cruz ✠, que en su frente ponemos. Por Cristo nuestro Señor.

℟: Amén.

Et hoc signum sanctae Crucis, ✠ quod nos fronti eius damus, tu, maledicte diabole, numquam audeas violare. Per eundem Christum Dominum nostrum.

℟ Amen.

Oremos.
Señor santo, Padre omnipotente, eterno Dios, autor de la luz y de la verdad, yo imploro tu piedad sobre este siervo tuyo *(esta sierva tuya)* N.., para que te dignes iluminarle*(la)* con la luz de tu inteligencia. Purifícale*(la)* y santifícale*(la)*, darle la ciencia verdadera, para que, hecho*(a)* digno*(a)* de la gracia de tu bautismo, conserve firme esperanza, recto consejo y santa doctrina. Por Cristo nuestro Señor.

℟: Amén.

Oremus.
Aeternam, ac iustissimam pietatem tuam deprecor, Domine, sancta, Pater omnipotens, aeterne Deus, auctor luminis et veritatis, super hunc famulum tuum *(hanc famulam tuam)* N.., ut digneris eum *(eam)* illuminare lumine intelligentiae tuae: munda eum *(eam)*, et sanctifica: da ei scientiam veram, ut, dignus *(-a)* gratia Baptismi tui effectus *(-a)*, teneat firmam spem, consilium rectum, doctrinam sanctam. Per Christum Dominum nostrum.

℟ Amen.

Ahora el sacerdote pone el extremo izquierdo de la estola sobre el infante y le conduce adentro del templo.
Todos siguen, mientras recen el Credo y el Pater Noster.

N.., ingredere in templum Dei, ut habeas partem cum Christo in vitam aeternam.
℟ Amen.

N.., entra en el templo de Dios, para que tengas parte con Cristo en la vida eterna.
℟: Amén.

Credo in Deum, Patrem omnipotentem, Creatorem caeli et terrae. Et in Iesum Christum, Filium eius unicum, Dominum nostrum: qui conceptus est de Spiritu Sancto, natus ex Maria Virgine, passus sub Pontio Pilato, crucifixus, mortuus, et sepultus: descendit ad inferos; tertia die resurrexit a mortuis; ascendit ad caelos; sedet ad dexteram Dei Patris omnipotentis; inde venturus est iudicare vivos et mortuos. Credo in Spiritum Sanctum, sanctam Ecclesiam catholicam, Sanctorum communionem, remissionem peccatorum, carnis resurrectionem, vitam aeternam. Amen.

Creo en Dios, Padre todopoderoso, creador del cielo y de la tierra. Creo en Jesucristo, su único Hijo, nuestro Señor, que fue concebido por obra y gracia del Espíritu Santo; nació de Santa María siempre Virgen; padeció bajo el poder de Poncio Pilato; fue crucificado, muerto y sepultado; descendió a los infiernos; al tercer día resucitó de entre los muertos; subió a los cielos y está sentado a la diestra de Dios Padre todopoderoso; desde allí ha de venir a juzgar a los vivos y a los muertos. Creo en el Espíritu Santo, la Santa Iglesia Católica, la comunión de los santos, el perdón de los pecados, la resurrección de la carne, y la vida eterna. Amén.

Padre nuestro que estás en los cielos: santificado sea tu nombre; venga a nosotros tu reino, hágase tu voluntad en la tierra como en el cielo.
El pan nuestro de cada día dánosle hoy, perdona nuestras deudas, así como nosotros perdonamos a nuestro deudores; y no nos dejes caer en la tentación mas líbranos del mal. Amén.

Pater noster, qui es in caelis, sanctificetur nomen tuum. Adveniat regnum tuum. Fiat voluntas tua, sicut in caelo, et in terra. Panem nostrum quotidianum da nobis hodie. Et dimitte nobis debita nostra, sicut et nos dimittimus debitoribus nostris. Et ne nos inducas in tentationem: sed libera nos a malo. Amen.

El sacerdote pronuncia después el siguiente exorcismo:

Exorcízote, inmundo espíritu, en el nombre de Dios ✠ Padre omnipotente, y en el nombre de Jesu ✠ cristo, su Hijo, Señor y Juez nuestro, y por la virtud del Espíritu ✠ Santo, para que te alejes de esta criatura de Dios N.., a la que el Señor se ha dignado llamar a su santo templo, para que se haga templo de Dios vivo y en él habite el Espíritu Santo. Por el mismo Cristo, nuestro Señor, que ha de venir a juzgar a los vivos y a los muertos, y al mundo por el fuego.
℟: Amén.

Exorcizo te, omnis spiritus immunde in nomine Dei ✠ Patris omnipotentis, et in nomine Iesu ✠ Christi Filii eius, Domini et Iudicis nostri, et in virtute Spiritus ✠ Sancti, ut discedas ab hoc plasmate Dei N.., quod Dominus noster ad templum sanctum suum vocare dignatus est, ut fiat templum Dei vivi, et Spiritus Sanctus habitet in eo. Per eundum Christum Dominum nostrum, qui venturus est iudicare vivos et mortuos, et saeculum per ignem.
℟ Amen.

El sacerdote, con el pulga de la derecha toma un poco de su saliva para tocar las orejas y la nariz del infante.

Ephpheta, quod est, Adaperire. In odorem suavitatis. Tu autem effugare, diabole; appropinquabit enim iudicium Dei.

Éfeta, que significa abríos. El olor de suavidad. Y tú diablo, huye, porque se acerca el juicio de Dios.

De nuevo pregunta a los padrinos quienes contestan en nombre del niño.

N.., abrenuntias Satanae?
℟ Abrenuntio.

Et omnibus operibus eius?
℟ Abrenuntio.

Et omnibus pompis eius?
℟ Abrenuntio.

N.., ¿renuncias a Satanás?
℟: Renuncio.

¿Y a todas sus obras?
℟: Renuncio.

¿Y a todas sus seducciones?
℟: Renuncio.

La madrina descubre un poco del pecho y de la espalda del infante. El sacerdote moja el pulgar con el Óleo de los Catechúmenos y unge al niño en el pecho y en la espalda.

Ego te linio ✠ oleo salutis in Christo Iesu Domino nostro, ut habeas vitam aeternam.
℟ Amen.

Yo te unjo ✠ con el óleo de la salud en Cristo nuestro Señor para que tengas la vida eterna.
℟: Amén.

Deja ya el sacerdote la estola morada y toma la estola blanca. Entra en el baptisterio, y con el los padrinos llevando al infante. Ante la pila el sacerdote hace las siguientes preguntas:

N.., ¿crees en Dios Padre omnipotente, creador del cielo y de la tierra?
℟: Creo.

N.., credis in Deum Patrem omnipotentem, creatorem caeli et terrae?
℟ Credo.

¿Crees en Jesucristo, su único Hijo, nuestro Señor, que nació y padeció?
℟: Creo.

Credis in Iesum Christum, Filium eius unicum, Dominum nostrum, natum, et passum?
℟ Credo.

¿Crees también en el Espíritu Santo, en la Santa Iglesia Católica, en la comunión de los Santos, en el perdón de los pecados, en la resurrección de la carne y en la vida eterna?
℟: Creo.

Credis et in Spiritum sanctum, sanctam Ecclesiam Catholicam, Sanctorum communionem, remissionem peccatorum, carnis resurrectionem, et vitam aeternam?
℟ Credo.

N.., ¿quieres ser bautizado*(a)*?
℟: Quiero.

N.., vis baptizari?
℟ Volo.

Los padrinos toman al niño en sus manos y le ponen de modo que el sacerdote cómodamente pueda derramar el agua bautismal sobre su frente. Mientras la derrama, haciendo por tres veces la señal de la cruz, dice el sacerdote:

N.., Ego te baptizo in nomine ✠ Patris, fundit primo, **et Filii ✠,** fundit secundo, **et Spiritus ✠ Sancti.** fundit tertio.

N.., yo te bautizo en el nombre del ✠ Padre, y del Hijo ✠, y del Espíritu ✠ Santo.

En seguida el sacerdote unge al infante con la Sagrada Crisma en la extremidad de la cabeza diciendo:

Deus omnipotens, Pater Domini nostri Iesu Christi, qui te regeneravit ex aqua et Spiritu Sancto, quique dedit tibi remissionem omnium peccatorum (hic inungit), ipse te ✠ liniat Chrismate Salutis in eodem Christo Iesu Domino nostro in vitam aeternam.
℟ Amen.

Dios omnipotente, Padre de nuestro Señor Jesucristo, que te ha regenerado por el agua y el Espíritu Santo y te ha perdonado todos tus pecados. El mismo te ✠ unja con el crisma de la salud en el mismo Jesucristo nuestro Señor, para la vida eterna.
℟ Amen.

Pax tibi.
℟ Et cum spiritu tuo.

La paz sea contigo.
℟: Y con tu espíritu.

Cubre el niño con un lienzo blanco diciendo:

Recibe la blanca vestidura y llévesela inmaculada ante el tribunal de nuestro Señor Jesucristo para que alcances la vida eterna.
℟: Amén.

Accipe vestem candidam, quam perferas immaculatam ante tribunal Domini nostri Iesu Christi, ut habeas vitam aeternam.
℟ Amen.

Luego el sacerdote da una vela encendida a los padrinos diciendo:

Recibe la lámpara encendida y guarda irreprensible tu bautismo; cumple los mandamientos de Dios; porque, cuando venga el Señor a las bodas, puedas salir a su encuentro en el cielo con todos sus Santos y vivas por los siglos de los siglos. Amén.

Accipe lampadem ardentem, et irreprehensibilis custodi Baptismum tuum: serva Dei mandata, ut, cum Dominus venerit ad nuptias, possis occurrere ei una cum omnibus Sanctis in aula caelesti, et vivas in saecula saeculorum.
℟ Amen.

N.., Vete en paz, y el Señor sea contigo.
℟: Amén.

N.., vade in pace, et Dominus sit tecum.
℟ Amen.

Consagración del niño a la Santísima Virgen María

DESPUÉS DEL BAUTISMO

Santísima Virgen María, Madre de Dios y Madre nuestra, te presentamos a este niño *(esta niña)* que Dios nos ha dado y confiado a nuestro cuidado y protección, y que hoy, por el Santo Bautismo, se ha hecho hijo *(hija)* de Dios y hermano*(a)* y miembro vivo de tu divino Hijo Jesús en la Santa Iglesia. Te lo *(la)* consagramos con todo nuestro corazón, y lo *(la)* entregamos confiadamente a tu ternura y vigilancia maternal.

Que por tu poderosa intercesión, Dios lo *(la)* proteja en su alma y en su cuerpo, y lo *(la)* preserve de todos los males. Si algún día tuviera la desgracia de pecar, recuérdale, Madre amorosísima, que ere bondadosa con el pecador arrepentido, y condúcelo*(la)* de nuevo a la gracia y amistad con tu divino Hijo.

Y a nosotros, sus padres y padrinos, ayúdanos a cumplir fielmente nuestras obligaciones con él *(ella)* y el compromiso que hemos contraído delante de Dios. Que con nuestra palabra y especialmente con nuestro ejemplo, le enseñemos a creer y practicar las verdades de la fe, el amor al prójimo, el cumplimiento de la Ley de Dios y el respeto a sus ministros.

Concédenos, finalmente, Santísima Virgen María, que algún día podamos juntarnos todos en la casa de nuestro Padre celestial, en la intimidad de tu Hijo y en el gozo del Espíritu Santo. Amén.

Admonición del bautismo

TOMADA DEL: EX MANUALI TOLETANO

Considerad diligentemente, hermanos, qué es lo que aquí hacemos. Celebramos el sacramento del Bautismo, que es en el orden de los sacramentos el primero, y en la dignidad y excelencia el grande, y que sin él ninguna persona puede alcanzar salud, según la sentencia del Salvador, que dijo a sus Apóstoles: *Id, enseñad a todas las gentes y bautizadlos en nombre del Padre y del Hijo y del Espíritu Santo: el que creyere y fuere bautizado, será salvo; y el que no creyere, será condenado.*

Por el Bautismo de agua y de Espíritu Santo somos reengendrados en nueva vida. Él es la puerta de todos los Sacramentos, y libra el alma de los males, que son verdaderos y grandes males, y acrecienta el caudal de los bienes. Porque todo pecado, sea original y el primero, o sea actual, por grave y enorme que sea, se perdona por la virtud y eficacia de este Sacramento: y la virtud de esta admirable agua, no solo quita la culpa del pecado, sino también por ella se perdona toda la pena que por él se debía. El alma se llena de gracia divina, por la cual hechos justos e hijos de Dios, somos nombrados por herederos de la vida eterna.

Llégase a estos bienes otro, que es el ornamento de las virtudes, que entra acompañando a la gracia, con que el alma se viste y atavía, y se junta e incorpora el bautizado con su Cabeza, que es Cristo nuestro Señor, hecho miembro del cuerpo místico de la Iglesia, en la cual Él como Cabeza preside: y de allí manan, como de viva y perpetua fuente, la gracia y todos los celestiales bienes; y sale una prontitud y habilidad grande para cumplir todas las obras de la vida cristiana. Y también se nos imprime en el alma una señal como Ovejas del rebaño de Cristo, la cual, como no se puede con ninguna fuerza humana borrar, hace este efecto, que el Sacramento del Bautismo una vez recibido, no se pueda, ni deba reiterar. Y finalmente, nos abre la puerta del Cielo que estaba cerrada por el pecado, para que entrando en la Gloria, gustemos de la vida bienaventurada, ajena de todas miserias.

ácense ceremonias muchas y graves en la administración del Bautismo por institución de los sagrados Apóstoles y Santos Padres: porque sus grandezas no sólo se signifiquen con palabras, sino con obras vivas que muevan los ojos, y de aquí se impriman más en la memoria. Los que se han de bautizar se detienen primero a las puertas de la Iglesia, porque son indignos de entrar en la Casa de Dios, antes que habiéndose despedido de la afrentosa servidumbre del demonio, se hayan juntado al imperio de Cristo. Dan sus nombres, para que se acuerden que son soldados de la bandera de Cristo, y profesan su milicia. Son instruidos con el santo Catecismo, según la institución de Cristo nuestro Señor, para que entiendan los que tienen edad, que es lo qué profesan, y a qué se obligan: y por los niños responden sus Padrinos.

Síguese el exorcismo, el cual se hace con palabras santas, y oraciones pías y religiosas para lanzar el demonio del ánima del Bautizado. Pónesele sal en la boca para que se libre de la corrupción del pecado, y para que reciba gusto y sabor de la sabiduría divina. Tócanle las orejas y narices con la saliva, a ejemplo del Ciego que Cristo nuestro Señor sanó, poniéndole lodo hecho con saliva en los ojos, al cual mandó que se los lavase con el agua de Síloe, que significaba el Bautismo. Úngesele con óleo santo y crisma, como a luchador, y para que se acuerde que es cristiano, y que en las costumbres y vida debe ser imitador de Cristo, de quien tiene el nombre de cristiano. Lo que significa la vestidura blanca y candela encendida que le dan, no hay para que decirlo; pues la misma ceremonia lo declara, que es advertir al bautizado, que guarde la pureza y blancura de la inocencia, y la claridad y luz de las buenas y santas obras. Estos frutos y efectos del Bautismo, y estas ceremonias habemos aquí declarado para que todos entiendan con que piedad y devoción se ha de recibir este Sacramento; y para que teniendo siempre en la memoria la profesión que en él hicieron, conozcan el beneficio y misericordia de Dios, que nos ha admitido a su santa fe, y a la fuente del Bautismo, sin algunos méritos nuestros, sino por su infinita bondad y benignidad: al cual sea dada toda honra y gloria en los siglos de los siglos. Amen.

℣. Adjutórium nostrum in nómine Dómini.

℟. Qui fecit cælum et terram.

PSALM 23

Antiphon

Hæc accípiet benedictiónem a Dómino, et misericórdiam a Deo salutári suo: quia hæc est generátio quæréntium Dóminum.

Dómini est terra, et plenitúdo ejus; * orbis terrárum, et univérsi, qui hábitant in eo.

Quia ipse super mária fundávit eum: * et super flúmina præparávit eum.

The Blessing of a Mother after Childbirth

ALSO KNOWN AS THE CHURCHING OF WOMEN

The priest greets the mother at the door of the church. She is kneeling and holding a lit candle.

He sprinkles her with holy water, then begins:

℣. Our help is in the Name of the Lord.
℟. Who made Heaven and Earth.

Ant. She shall receive a blessing from the Lord, and mercy from God her Savior: for this is the generation of them that seek the Lord.

The Earth is the Lord's and the fullness thereof, * the world and all they that dwell therein.

For He hath founded it upon the seas, * and hath prepared it upon the rivers.

Who shall ascend into the mountain of the Lord, * or who shall stand in His holy place?

Bendición de la mujer después del parto

El sacerdote, revestido de sobrepelliz y estola blanca, y acompañado del ministro con el acetre e hisopo, se dirige a la puerta de la iglesia, donde aguarda la mujer, arrodillada, teniendo en la mano una vela encendida.

El sacerdote la rocía con agua bendita. Luego dice:

℣. Nuestro auxilio está en el nombre del Señor.

℟. Que hizo el cielo y la tierra.

Ant. Esta mujer recibirá la bendición del Señor y la misericordia de Dios, su Salvador, porque es una de las que buscan al Señor.

Del Señor es la tierra y cuanto ella contiene; * el mundo y todos sus habitadores.

Porque Él la estableció superior a los mares, * y la colocó más alto que los ríos.

¿Quién subirá al monte del Señor? * ¿O quién podrá estar en su Santuario?

Quis ascéndet in montem Dómini, *
aut quis stabit in loco sancto ejus?

Innocens mánibus, et mundo corde, *
qui non accépit in vano ánimam suam,
nec jurávit in dolo próximo suo.

Hic accípiet benedictiónem a Dómino:
*et misericórdiam a Deo salutári suo.

Hæc est generátio quæréntium eum, *
quæréntium fáciem Dei Jacob.

Attóllite portas, príncipes, vestras, et elevámini portæ æternáles: * et introíbit Rex glóriæ.

Quis est iste Rex glóriæ ? * Dóminus fortis, et potens; Dóminus potens in prœlio.

Attóllite portas, príncipes, vestras, et elevámini portæ æternáles: * et introíbit Rex glóriæ.

Quis est iste Rex gloriæ? * Dóminus virtútum, ipse est Rex gloriæ.

Glória Patri, et Fílio, * et Spíritui Sancto.
Sicut erat in princípio, et nunc, et semper, * et in saécula sæculórum. Amen.

Ant. Hæc accípiet benedictiónem a Dómino, et misericórdiam a Deo salutári suo: quia hæc est generátio quæréntium Dóminum.

The innocent in hands and clean of heart, who hath not taken his soul in vain, * nor sworn deceitfully to his neighbor.

He shall receive a blessing from the Lord, * and mercy from God his Savior.

This is the generation of them that seek Him, * of them that seek the face of the God of Jacob.

Lift up your gates, O ye princes, and be ye lifted up, O eternal gates, * and the King of glory shall enter in!

"Who is this King of glory?" * "the Lord Who is strong and mighty, the Lord mighty in battle."

Lift up your gates, O ye princes, and be ye lifted up, O eternal gates, * and the King of glory shall enter in!

"Who is this King of glory?" * "the Lord of hosts, He is the King of glory."

Glory be to the Father, and to the Son, * and to the Holy Ghost.

As it was in the beginning, is now, and ever shall be, * world without end. Amen.

Ant. She shall receive a blessing from the Lord, and mercy from God her Savior: for this is the generation of them that seek the Lord.

El que tiene puras las manos y limpio el corazón; el que no dirige su mente hacia cosas vanas, * ni ha hecho juramentos engañosos a su prójimo.

Este es el que recibirá la bendición del Señor * y la recompensa de Dios, su Salvador.

Tal es el linaje de los que le buscan, * de los que anhelan por ver el rostro del Dios de Jacob.

Levantad, oh puertas, vuestras cabezas, y elevaos vosotros, oh portales antiguos, * para que entre el rey de la gloria.

"¿Quién es ese rey de la gloria?"* "Es el Señor fuerte y poderoso; el Señor poderoso en las batallas."

Levantad, puertas, vuestras cabezas, y elevaos vosotros, oh portales antiguos, * para que entre el rey de la gloria.

"¿Quién es ese rey de la gloria?" * El Señor de los ejércitos, ése es el rey de la gloria.

Gloria al Padre, y al Hijo, * y al Espíritu Santo.

Como era en el principio, ahora y siempre, * y por los siglos de los siglos. Amén.

Ant. Esta mujer recibirá la bendición del Señor y la misericordia de Dios, su Salvador, porque es una de las que buscan al Señor.

Ingrédere in templum Dei, adóra
Fílium beátæ Maríæ Vírginis,
qui tibi fecunditátem tríbuit prolis.

Kyrie eléison.
Christe eléison.
Kyrie eléison.
Pater noster… (Secreto)

℣. Et ne nos indúcas in tentatiónem.
℟. Sed líbera nos a malo.

℣. Salvam fac ancílliam tuam, Dómine.
℟. Deus meus, sperántem in te.

℣. Mitte ei, Dómine, auxílium de sancto.
℟. Et de Sion tuére eam.

℣. Nihil profíciat inimícus in ea.

℟. Et fílius iniquitátis non appónat nocére ei.

℣. Dómine, exáudi oratiónem meam.
℟. Et clamor meus ad te véniat.

℣. Dóminus vobíscum.
℟. Et cum spíritu tuo.

The priest now guides the mother into the church by the edge of his stole, saying:

Enter into the temple of God, adore the Son of the blessed Virgin Mary, who gave you fruitfulness of offspring.

The mother kneels at the altar rail. The priest continues:

Lord, have mercy.
Christ, have mercy.
Lord, have mercy.
Our Father… (recited silently)

℣. And lead us not into temptation.
℟. But deliver us from evil.

℣. Save your handmaid, Lord.
℟. Who hopes in Thee, my God.

℣. Send her help, Lord, from the sanctuary.
℟. And defend her out of Sion.

℣. Let not the enemy prevail against her.
℟. Nor the son of iniquity approach to hurt her.
℣. O Lord, hear my prayer.
℟. And let my cry come unto Thee.

℣. The Lord be with you.
℟. And with thy spirit.

Después, poniendo en la mano de la mujer la extremidad izquierda de la estola, la introduce en la iglesia, diciendo:

Entre en el Templo de Dios, adora al Hijo de la bienaventurada Virgen María, que te ha concedido la fecundidad de la prole.

Habiendo entrado, la mujer se arrodilla ante el altar. Luego el sacerdote dice:

Señor, ten piedad.
Cristo, ten piedad.
Señor, ten piedad.
Padre nuestro…(en silencio)

℣. Y no nos dejes caer en la tentación.

℟. Mas líbranos del mal.

℣. Salva, Señor, a tu sierva.

℟. Dios mío, que espera en Ti

℣. Envíale, Señor, socorro desde tu Santuario.

℟. Y protégela desde de la Sión celestial.

℣. El enemigo no obtenga sobre ella ninguna ventaja.

℟. Y el hijo de la iniquidad no logre dañarle.

℣. Señor, oye mi oración.

℟. Y llegue hasta Ti mi súplica.

℣. El Señor sea con vosotros.

℟. Y con tu espíritu.

Orémus.
Omnípotens sempitérne Deus, qui per beátæ Maríæ Vírginis partum fidélium pariéntium dolóres in gáudium vertísti: réspice propítius super hanc fámulam tuam, ad templum sanctum tuum pro gratiárum actióne lætam accedéntem, et præsta; ut post hanc vitam, ejúsdem beátæ Maríæ méritis et intercessióne, ad ætérnæ beatitúdinis gáudia cum prole sua perveníre mereátur. Per Christum Dóminum nostrum.
℟. Amen.

Pax et benedíctio Dei omnipoténtis, Patris, et Fílii, ✠ et Spíritus Sancti, descéndat super te, et máneat semper.
℟. Amen.

Let us pray.
Almighty, everlasting God, through the delivery of the blessed Virgin Mary, Thou hast turned into joy the pains of the faithful in childbirth; look mercifully upon this Thy handmaid, coming in gladness to Thy temple to offer up her thanks: and grant that after this life, by the merits and intercession of the same blessed Mary, she may merit to arrive, together with her offspring, at the joys of everlasting happiness. Through Christ our Lord

℟. Amen.

Oremos:
Omnipotente y sempiterno Dios, que, mediante el parto de la Bienaventurada virgen María convertiste en gozo los dolores de las cristianas que dan a luz: mira propicio a esta tu sierva, que viene alegre a tu santo templo para darte gracias, y haz que, después de esta vida, por los méritos e intercesión de la misma Bienaventurada María, logre conseguir juntamente con su prole los goces de la eterna bienaventuranza. Por Cristo Señor nuestro.

℟. Amén.

The priest sprinkles the mother with holy water in the form of a cross and then he blesses her:

Finalmente, la rocía de nuevo con agua bendita en forma de cruz. Luego dice:

The peace and blessing of God almighty, the Father, and the Son, ✠ and the Holy Spirit, descend upon you and remain forever.
℟. Amen.

La paz y la bendición de Dios omnipotente, Padre, e Hijo ✠, y Espíritu Santo, descienda sobre ti y permanezca siempre.
℟. Amén.

REFUGIUM
PECCATORUM
VENEZ TOUS A MOI, ET
JE VOUS PROTÉGERAI
AVE
MARIA
COR
MARIÆ
IMMACULATÆ

Another Consecration of a Child to Our Lady

AFTER THE RECEPTION OF HOLY BAPTISM

At the altar of Our Lady, the godmother holding the newly baptized child, all recite a Hail Mary. Then the parents or the priest prays the following prayer:

Holy Mary, Mother of God and mother of all the faithful, I place this little child under your mothering protection. To you I consecrate it, body and soul.

Take it under your care and keep it always. Protect it in its infancy and keep it sound in body and mind. Guard over its youth and keep its heart pure, its thought ever holy and directed to God and spiritual things.

Protect it always throughout life, in its joys and sorrows, in its successes and failures, in its dealings with others. Always and in all things be a true Mother to it, Mary, and preserve it.
I recommend it entirely to you.

Remember, Mother Mary, that through this act of consecration it is by a special claim your child; guard it and keep it as your property and possession. Amen.

The priest continues:

℣ Adjutórium nostrum in nómine Dómini.	℣. Our help is in the Name of the Lord.
℟ Qui fecit cælum et terram.	℟. Who made Heaven and Earth.

℣ Dóminus vobíscum.
℟ Et cum spíritu tuo.

Oremus.

Defende, quæsumus, Dómine, beatæ Mariæ semper Vírginis intercedente, istam ab omni adversitáte famíliam; et toto corde tibi prostrátam, ab hostium propítius tuére cleménter insídiis. Per Jesum Christum Dominum nostrum. Amen.

℣. The Lord be with you.
℟. And with thy spirit.

Let us pray.
Defend, we beseech Thee, O Lord, this family from all adversity, through the intercession of the Blessed Mary ever Virgin; and as it is prostrate before Thee with all its heart, mercifully protect it from the snares of the enemy. Through Jesus Christ our Lord. Amen.

Conclude with the Salve Regina.

www.ingramcontent.com/pod-product-compliance
Lightning Source LLC
LaVergne TN
LVHW052309100826
845147LV00006B/711

* 9 7 8 1 7 3 2 7 9 3 6 2 0 *